Good
Character
Traits

I0164846

Resilience

Ashley Lee

Explore other books at:
WWW.ENGAGEBOOKS.COM

VANCOUVER, B.C.

e → WWW.ENGAGEBOOKS.COM

Resilience: Good Character Traits
Lee, Ashley, 1995 –
Text © 2025 Engage Books
Design © 2025 Engage Books

Edited by: A.R. Roumanis
Design by: Mandy Christiansen

Text set in Myriad Pro Regular.
Chapter headings set in Anton.

FIRST EDITION / FIRST PRINTING

LIBRARY AND ARCHIVES CANADA CATALOGUING IN PUBLICATION

Title: Resilience / Ashley Lee.
Names: Lee, Ashley, author.
Description: Series statement: Good Character Traits

ISBN 978-1-77878-725-6 (hardcover)
ISBN 978-1-77878-731-7 (softcover)

This project has been made possible in part
by the Government of Canada.

Canada

Resilience

Contents

What Is Resilience?

Resilience is when someone is able to feel good again after going through hard times.

It means being strong and never giving up.

Resilience is about learning to deal with problems.

Why Is Resilience Important?

Resilience helps people grow and learn.

It helps them become even stronger.

What Does Resilience Look Like?

Resilient people believe in themselves when things get hard.

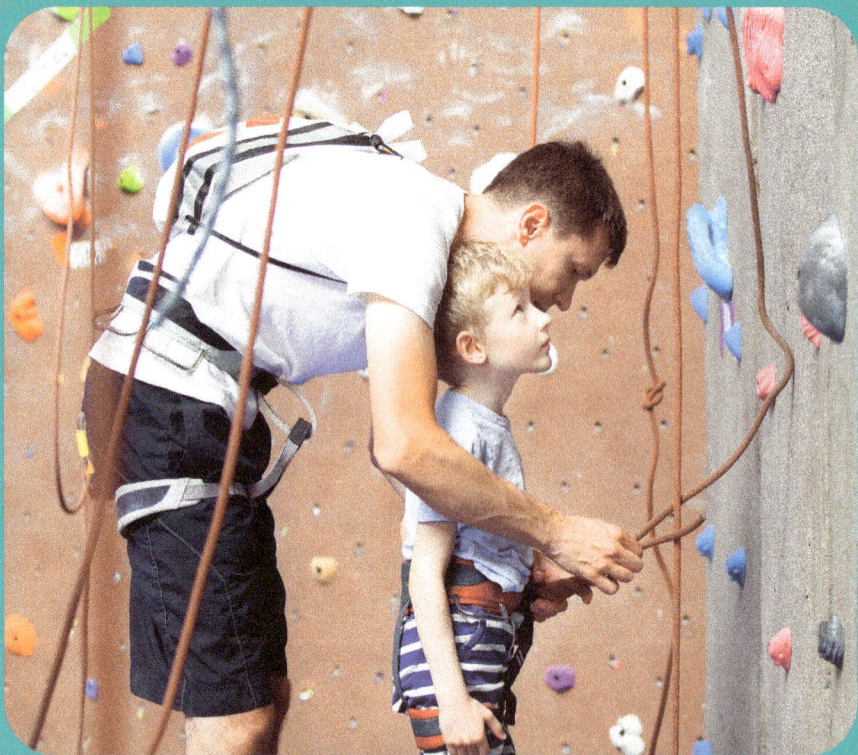

They are able to feel good about what might happen in the future.

How Does Resilience Affect You?

Resilience can make your **mental health** better.

> **Key Word**
>
> **Mental health:** the health of your mind.

It helps you feel good about yourself and your **abilities**.

Key Word

Abilities: power to do things.

How Does Resilience Affect Others?

Being resilient shows others that they can be resilient too.

They may be **inspired** by you and your resilience.

Key Word

Inspired: made to want to do something.

Resilience

Is Everyone Resilient?

Not everyone is resilient. But everyone is able to be resilient.

It often takes **practice** to become more resilient.

Key Word

Practice: do something over and over again to get better at it.

Is It Bad if You Are Not Resilient?

It is not bad if you are not resilient. Everyone is different.

Ask for help if you are going through a hard time.

Asking for help is a sign that you are strong.

Does Resilience Change Over Time?

You become more resilient every time you go through something hard.

You are able to learn from what happened and grow over time.

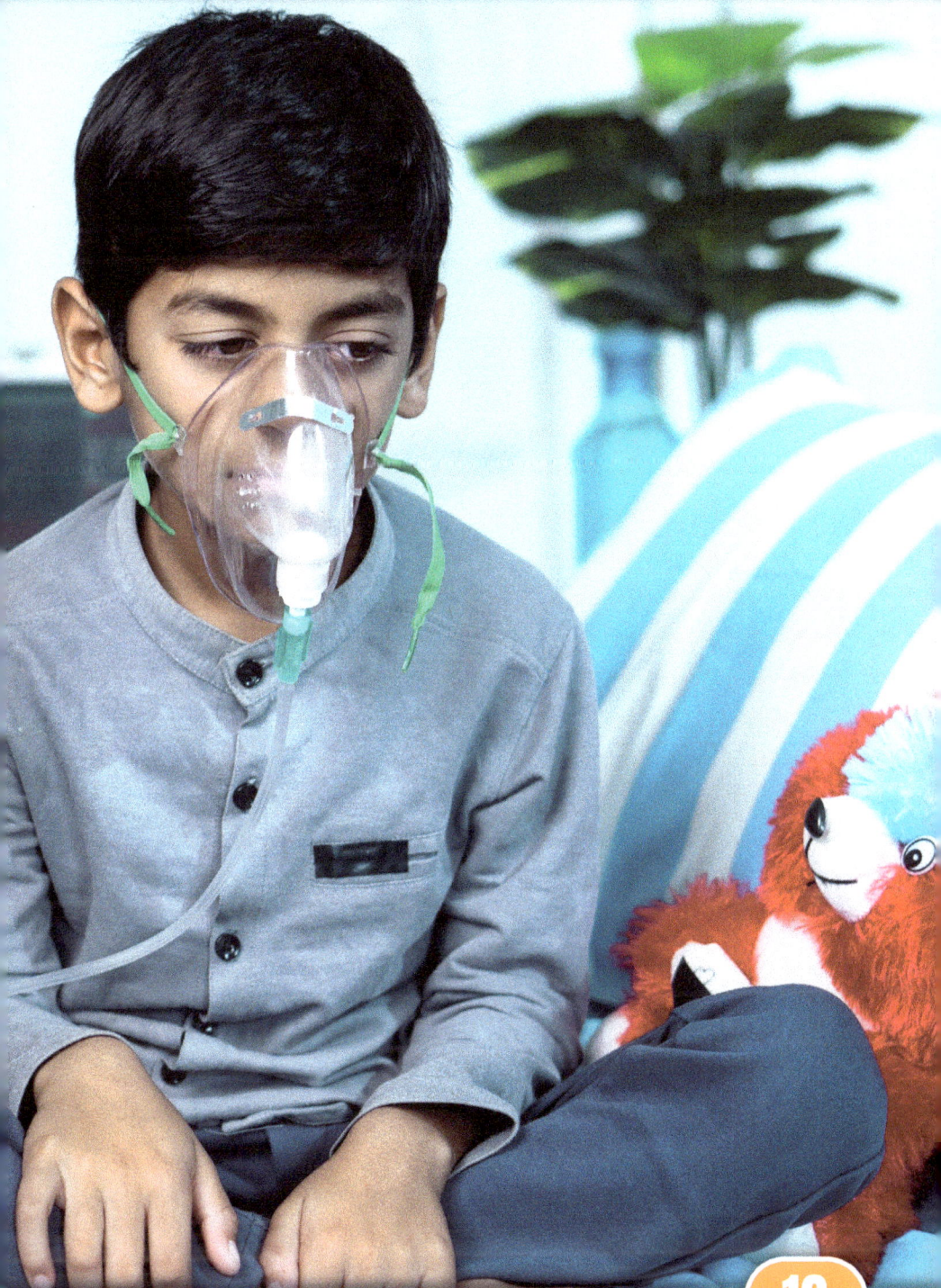

Is It Hard to Be Resilient?

It takes a lot of work to become resilient.

But it can get easier
with time and practice.

How Can You Learn to Be More Resilient?

Try to think about ways to make your problems better.

Try to learn something every time you go through something hard.

How Can You Help Others Be More Resilient?

Be there for other people. Listen to their problems.

Talk about a time you went through something hard. This can give them **hope**.

Key Word

Hope: when someone believes something will happen.

How to Be Resilient Every Day

1. Know that not all change is bad.
2. Do not wait for problems to go away on their own.

3. Set **goals** for yourself.

4. Check in with your feelings during the day.

Key Word

Goals: things that people want that they work hard to get.

Resilience Around the World

People had to stay away from others during the COVID-19 **pandemic**.

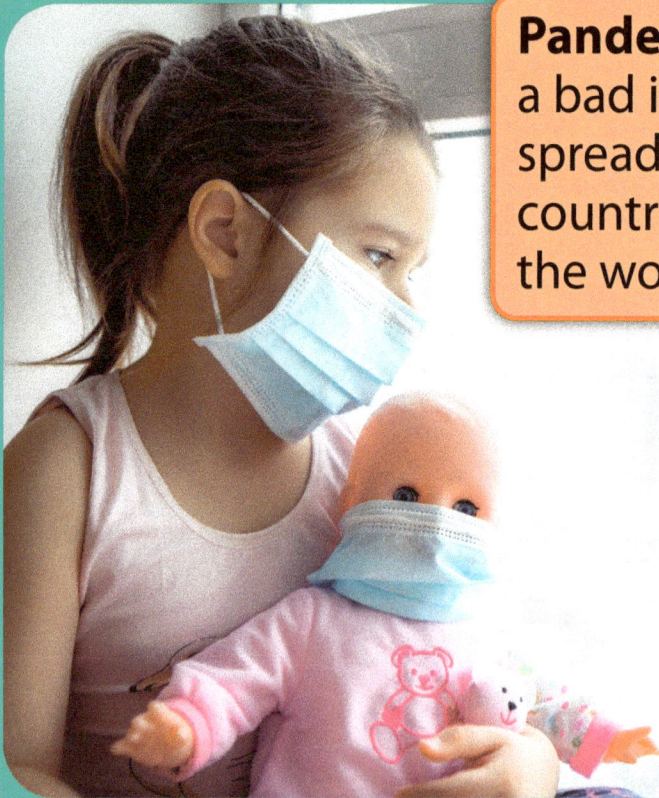

Key Word

Pandemic: when a bad illness spreads to many countries around the world.

People all over the world were resilient. They found new ways to stay connected.

Many people talked to each other on the computer during this time.

Quiz

Test your knowledge of resilience by answering the following questions. The questions are based on what you have read in this book. The answers are listed on the bottom of the next page.

2 Can resilience make your mental health better?

1 Does resilience help people grow and learn?

3 Is everyone resilient?

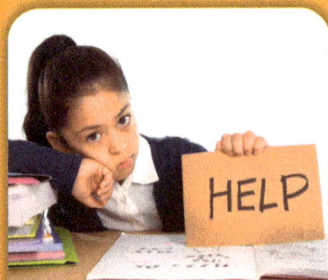

5 Does it take a lot of work to become resilient?

4 Is asking for help a sign that you are strong?

6 Is all change bad?

Explore Other Level 1 Readers.

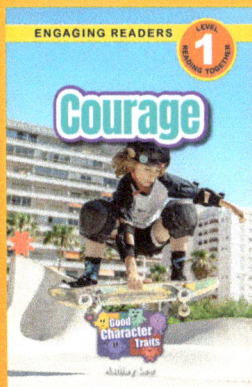
ENGAGING READERS — LEVEL 1 — Courage — Good Character Traits — Ashley Lee

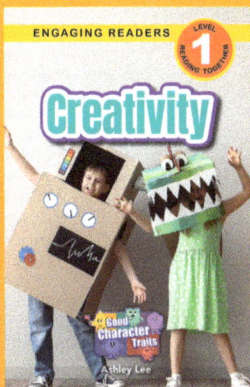
ENGAGING READERS — LEVEL 1 — Creativity — Good Character Traits — Ashley Lee

ENGAGING READERS — LEVEL 1 — Positivity — Good Character Traits — Ashley Lee

ENGAGING READERS — LEVEL 1 — Respect — Good Character Traits — Ashley Lee

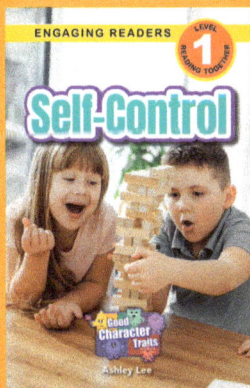
ENGAGING READERS — LEVEL 1 — Self-Control — Good Character Traits — Ashley Lee

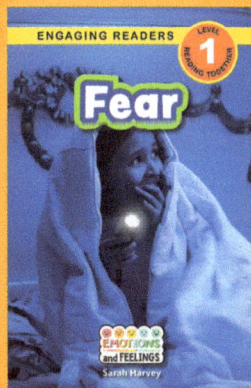
ENGAGING READERS — LEVEL 1 — Fear — Emotions and Feelings — Sarah Harvey

ENGAGING READERS — LEVEL 1 — Happiness — Emotions and Feelings — Sarah Harvey

ENGAGING READERS — LEVEL 1 — Sadness — Emotions and Feelings — Sarah Harvey

ENGAGING READERS — LEVEL 1 — Surprise — Emotions and Feelings — Sarah Harvey

Visit www.engagebooks.com/readers

www.ingramcontent.com/pod-product-compliance
Lightning Source LLC
Chambersburg PA
CBHW052036030426
42337CB00027B/5031